Simple Starter
Crochet Projects

3 EASY PATTERNS FOR YOUR FIRST HAT, SCARF, AND CUSHION

T0284462

Carol Meldrum

Landauer Publishing

Simple Starter Crochet Projects

Landauer Publishing, www.landauerpub.com, is an imprint of Fox Chapel Publishing Company, Inc.

Copyright © 2010, 2024 Carol Meldrum and Fox Chapel Publishing Company, Inc., 903 Square Street, Mount Joy, PA 17552.

Simple Starter Crochet Projects (ISBN 978-1-63981-060-4) contains content first published in 2010 by New Holland Publishers (UK) Ltd in the book *Love... Crochet.*

Project Team
Managing Editor: Gretchen Bacon
Acquisitions Editor: Amelia Johanson
Editor: Christa Oestreich
Designer: Wendy Reynolds

Shutterstock used: Coxy Home (back cover), Oleksandr Nagaiets (page 5), APN Photography (page 10).

ISBN 978-1-63981-060-4

The Cataloging-in-Publication Data is on file with the Library of Congress.

We are always looking for talented authors. To submit an idea, please send a brief inquiry to acquisitions@foxchapelpublishing.com.

Note to Professional Copy Services:
The publisher grants you permission to make up to six copies of any quilt patterns in this book for any customer who purchased this book and states the copies are for personal use.

Printed in China
First printing

Contents

28

32

36

Introduction 4

THE BASICS 6
 Tools 8
 Yarns 10
 Getting Started 11
 Basic Stitch Techniques 12
 Working in the Round 16
 Front and Back Posts 17
 Shaping Techniques 19
 Crocheting in the Back Loop. 20
 Corded Edge 21
 Understanding Tension 22
 Following the Instructions 23
 Understanding Patterns 23
 Seams 24

THE PROJECTS. 26
 Narrow Stripe Beret 28
 Chunky Chevron Hooded Scarf 32
 Outdoor Cushion 36

Index. 39

Crochet Hook Conversion Chart 40

Table of Abbreviations. 40

Introduction

The craft of crochet is quite young compared to other needlecrafts, such as weaving and knitting. Historically, crochet was used in the mid-19th century to recreate the look of expensive European laces, and during Queen Victoria's reign, it was widely used in clothing and household wares. Today, once again, crochet is as popular as ever for both pleasure and practical purposes. While continuing traditions of the past, we can enjoy delving into tried and tested techniques, dipping into stitches, and mixing them up with modern yarns and colors to give crochet a 21st century update.

It's incredibly easy to get started with crochet because it involves a repetition of the same movement. You're simply drawing yarn through a loop on a the hook, so the basics are quick to pick up. It can feel a little strange to start off, especially if you are used to knitting, but the fingers soon learn the new movements and the rhythm becomes like a calming second nature. The projects featured are quick to make, often taking only take a few evenings to produce. You can easily carry your hook and yarn with you wherever you go, making it perfect for filling in those pockets of free time throughout the day. All the essential techniques you need are explained in detail at the beginning of the book, and close-up photos of the projects show the stitch details, making them simple to follow.

Whether you are a complete beginner or already a crochet pro, by working through the projects, you will learn new skills. And, ultimately, what could be better than adding individuality to your outfit with a one-off fashion piece or real style to your home!

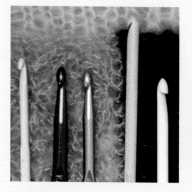  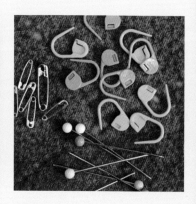

The Basics

Tools

You don't need much equipment to get started. The essentials are a hook, some yarn, and a pair of sharp scissors. Other equipment can simply be added to your collection along the way.

Hooks. There is a wide variety of crochet hooks to choose from, and it is a matter of personal choice as to the type of hook you prefer to use. The most commonly used hook is either aluminum or plastic. Smaller steel sizes are used for working with fine crochet threads, and other aluminum hooks have plastic or soft handles to give a better grip, making it a bit easier on the fingers. Bamboo and birchwood hooks have a very smooth finish and often have pretty decorative handles, which add to their appeal.

Hooks also come in a range of sizes from very thin to very thick. It tends to be the rule that thinner hooks are used for finer yarns and thicker hooks are used for thicker yarns, but you can have fun playing with this once you know what you are doing.

Hooks are sized according to their thickness, either in a number or letter system depending on the brand (see page 40). The different parts that make up the hook—the point, the throat, the thumb rest, and the handle—can vary from brand to brand, so try different types to see which one suits you best.

Whichever hook you choose, it's important to look after your tools. It's a good idea to invest in a hook roll with pockets or, alternatively, loops to keep everything in place. Or you could simply use a pencil case to keep things tidy.

Pins. The glass-headed pin is a good all-rounder to have. They are the best type to use when blocking and pressing because plastic and pearl-headed pins can melt with the heat.

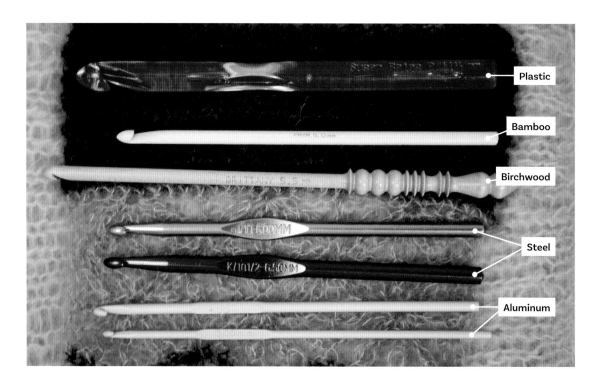

Plastic

Bamboo

Birchwood

Steel

Aluminum

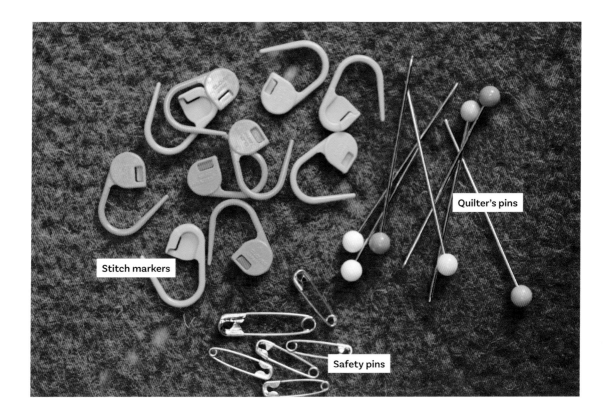

Quilter's pins

Stitch markers

Safety pins

Quilter's pins can also be useful when pinning pieces together as they tend not to fall out so easily, but generally I find that you can't go wrong with plain old safety pins.

Scissors. Small, pointed scissors are good for cutting and trimming ends and you may find that they also fit snugly in your hook case.

Sewing needles. The main type of needle needed is a tapestry or yarn needle, which will have a blunt point and a long eye for threading thicker yarns through. They come in a variety of sizes and are the best type of needle for weaving in ends and sewing up crochet fabrics.

Stitch markers. These are very useful to have in your kit. They are usually brightly colored plastic split rings or shaped loops that easily slip into and around your crochet stitches without splitting the yarn. They are usually used to highlight the beginning of a repeat or indicate the end of a round.

Tape measure. Choose one that shows both inches and centimeters on the same side. A 12" (30.5cm) metal or plastic ruler is also good for measuring your tension.

Yarns

There are so many different yarns on the market, from shiny mercerized cottons to hairy eyelash yarns, making everything from rough, bumpy textures to smooth, evenly spun strands. In theory you can crochet with any continuous length of fiber, but it is important to understand the fiber content and texture of the yarn as this will affect the finished look and quality of the fabric.

Yarns are created by spinning fibers together. These can be natural fibers, from plants and animals like wool and cotton, or they can be manmade or synthetic fibers like nylon or acrylic. Yarns can also be made up of a single fiber or by a blend of different fibers. The various thicknesses of yarns or plies are made up of finer strands twisted together to form the different weights used. Textured and tweedy yarns are often created by twisting several strands of different thicknesses and colors together, giving a whole new look. Other yarns are formed slightly differently; ribbon yarns are constructed by knitting a very fine yarn into a tube, giving a rounded or flat appearance on the ball. However, when starting out with crochet, it is best to go for a yarn that has a smooth surface and a tight twist.

Generally, yarn is purchased by weight rather than length and is packaged in balls, hanks, or skeins. The length of the yarn is an important piece of information, especially when you need to substitute one for another, and most brands will give you this information on the ball band. The way in which a yarn is spun can also affect the length. When using hanks or skeins, they need to be wound up into balls before they are used to crochet.

Animal fibers. Wool is the most commonly used animal fiber, and although all wool comes from sheep, there are still a variety of qualities. Merino wool is made from superfine fibers and is very soft and robust, whereas scratchier wools tend to come from sheep that have

longer, shaggier coats. Other animal fibers also include mohair and cashmere, which comes from goats, and angora from rabbits and alpacas. Silk is also classed as a natural fiber; it comes from the unwound cocoons of silkworms spun to make a yarn that has a soft, shiny luster. It is also a very strong and light yarn but can be an expensive choice.

Plant fibers. Cotton and linen are the most commonly used plant fibers. Cotton really lends itself to crochet and, like wool, it comes in different forms. Different plants produce different types of fibers: cotton can be matte and soft, or if you want a bit of a shine, mercerized cotton has a similar appearance to silk. Linen, bamboo, and hemp are among the other yarns spun from plant fibers. Linen has a crisp feel and is spun from the fibers of the flax plant. It has a slightly waxy feel on the ball, but drapes beautifully and feels cool to wear. It's also environmentally friendly—as is hemp.

Synthetic fibers. Acrylic, nylon, and polyester are all made from synthetic fibers. They are processed from coal- and petroleum-based products, so are essentially the same thing as plastic. Yarns made from 100% synthetic fibers are a lot less expensive, making them a good choice if you are on a budget, but it's best to use one that has at least some natural fiber mixed in if possible. This makes the yarn much nicer to work with and will also give the fabric a more elastic property, helping it to keep its shape.

Getting Started

Learning a new skill is great fun, but it is important to understand the basics before starting a project. Work your way through the techniques here, making practice swatches of each of the different stitches. When you come across a new technique in a project, it's a good idea to give it a quick practice first on some spare yarn.

Holding the Hook

There are a couple of different methods for holding the hook. There is no real right or wrong way, but the most important choice is to use the method that's the most comfortable and works best for you. The hook is usually held in the right hand.

Method 1: Hold the hook as if it were a pencil. The tips of your right thumb and should rest over the flat section of the hook.

Method 2: Hold the hook as if it were a knife, grasping the flat section of the hook between your thumb and forefinger.

Holding the Yarn

Again, there is no definitive way to hold the yarn, but it should easily feed through your fingers, allowing you to create a slight tension that helps keep your stitches nice and even.

Method 1: Loop the short end of the yarn over the left forefinger. The end of the yarn coming from the ball should be under the next finger. Grip the length of yarn toward the ball of yarn gently with your fingers.

Method 2: As before, the short end of the yarn should be over your left forefinger. The end of the yarn coming from the ball should be under your next finger, but then also over the next. Some people also like to wrap the yarn around their little finger in this technique.

Basic Stitch Techniques

Making the First Loop

Every crochet stitch starts and ends with one loop on the hook. All crochet is made up from a series of loops, and the first loop begins as a slip knot. Remember, this first loop does not count as an actual stitch.

1 Take the end of yarn in your right hand and wrap around your forefinger on the left hand in a cross. Turn your finger so that the cross is facing downward.

2 Take the crochet hook in your left hand. Place it under the first loop on your left forefinger and draw through the second loop.

3 Remove your finger and pull both ends of yarn firmly.

Making a Foundation Chain

The chain is the starting point for nearly all pieces of crochet fabric and is where you work your first row of stitches. The chain is made up connecting loops, and since you need to be able to fit your hook back into the chain, be careful not to make it too tight.

1 Hold your hook in the right hand and yarn in the left. Gently grip the base of the slip knot just under the hook with your thumb and forefinger. This will stop the loop from twirling freely around your hook when you work the chain.

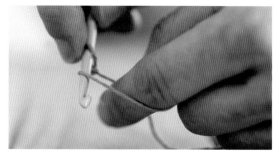

2 Take the hook and place it under the strand of yarn that runs from your hook and over your left-hand forefinger. This is described in patterns as a yarn over, but it is really worked as hook under yarn. Turn the hook with your fingers so the hook part is now facing down. This movement will grab the strand of yarn and allow the hook to move fairly easily back through the loop. Bring the hook back through the loop toward yourself.

3 Slide the loop that you have just made up the shaft of the hook. The neck is much narrower here than the shaft, so if you keep the loop on the neck, it will be too tight. Use your right-hand forefinger to anchor the stitch, and slightly stretch the yarn with your left-hand fingers.

Work from steps 2 and 3 to create the length of chain required for the project. As you work the chain, move your left-hand fingers up, keeping them at the base of the chain just worked.

Counting Chains

Each V-shaped loop on the front of the chain counts as one, except the one on the hook, which is a working stitch.

Turning Chains

When working crochet, you need to work a specific number of extra chains at the beginning of a row. These stitches are called turning chains and bring the hook up to the correct height ready for the next stitch to be worked. This ensures the fabric keeps a straight edge. As a rule, the longer the stitch, the longer the turning chain.
  - Single crochet—1 turning chain
  - Half double crochet—2 turning chains
  - Double crochet—3 turning chains
  - Treble—4 turning chains
  - Double treble—5 turning chains

Slip Stitch (sl st)

The slip stitch is a very useful stitch and is basically a chain that has been connected to the work. Slip stitches are normally used to link a stitch or group of stitches to another point, or they are used or to move along a row you are working on without having to break off the yarn and rejoin it further along. They are also commonly used when working flat motifs or tubes to join the rows into rounds.

1 Insert the hook into the stitch. Make sure the hook is under both parts of the stitch.

2 Yarn over and draw through both loops on hook (2 loops on hook) to complete the stitch.

Single Crochet (sc)

This is the easiest of crochet fabrics to create. The stitch is good to use in projects that require a compact fabric that you want to be flexible but not too stretchy, like hats and bags. It's also used in basic borders, trims, and ties.

Once you have worked the length of chain required, work one extra chain. This is your turning chain.

3 Using the hook, draw the loop back through the chain toward yourself. You should now have two loops on the hook.

1 Using the top point of the hook, insert it from front to back into the second chain from the hook. Remember not to count the loop on your hook as a stitch.

4 Finish the stitch by doing a yarn over again and drawing through both loops on the hook. You should be left with one loop on your hook. Once you have completed your first stitch, continue along the chain working 1sc (single crochet) into each chain to the end. Start each stitch by inserting your hook into the center of the next chain.

At the end of the row, turn your fabric so you are ready to start a new row. Always work turning stitches at the beginning of each row.

2 Using the same method as when making the foundation chain, place the yarn around the hook, then turn the hook so that it faces downward to catch the yarn.

Double crochet (dc)

The double crochet is a longer stitch than the single, which creates a more open fabric. It is used frequently in many open lace fabrics.

    The stitch is worked in a similar way to the single, except the yarn is wrapped around the hook before working into the fabric. Once you have worked the length of chain required, work three extra chains. This is your turning chain.

1 Before working into the chain, wrap the yarn around the hook as if you were going to work a chain, but do not pull the loop through.

2 Count four chains along from the hook, and insert the hook into this chain. The first three chains are your turning chain, so the place where you insert your hook will be the position of your first stitch. Using the same method as when making a foundation chain, place the yarn around the hook, then turn the hook so it faces downward to catch the yarn.

3 Using the hook, draw the loop back through the chain toward yourself. You should now have three loops on your hook.

4 Place the yarn around the hook again, and draw through the first two loops on hook. You should now have two loops on your hook.

5 Finish the stitch by placing the yarn around the hook again, and draw through both loops. There is now one loop left on the hook and the stitch is complete. Once you have completed your first stitch, continue along the chain, working 1dc (double crochet) into each chain to the end. Start each stitch by doing a yarn over before inserting your hook into the center of the next chain.

At the end of the row, turn your fabric so you are ready to start a new row. Always work turning stitches at the beginning of each row.

Working in the Round

Some crochet projects are worked in rounds rather than in rows. This means that you crochet around the work rather than working back and forth in rows, changing from front to back each time.

Making a Ring

This is the first step for working in the round. The ring is usually made up of a small number of chains with the ends joined together with a slip stitch to form the ring.

1 Chain six, and insert the hook from front to back into the first chain made.

2 Wrap the yarn around the hook, and draw back through the chain and the loop on your hook. Gently tighten by pulling the loose end of yarn.

Increasing in the Round

To keep a circular piece of crochet flat, you have to increase evenly around the outer edge of your work; the number of stitches you increase by in each round will depend on the amount worked in the first round. For example, if you worked 10 stitches into the ring, then you will increase by a multiple of 10 each time. On the first round, you increase into every stitch; on the second round, you increase on every second stitch; and so on.

Working into the Ring

The ring forms the center of your work, and by working into the ring, you form the first round. When working into the ring, watch that you don't work back over the first stitches, especially when the pattern asks for a large number of stitches and the ring isn't very big. Depending on the stitch you will be working, make the appropriate length of turning chain. This example is worked in single crochet, so one extra chain has been used.

1 Insert the hook from front to back through the center of the ring. With the yarn around hook, pull back and draw through two loops.

2 Once you have worked the correct number of stitches, complete the round by joining the ends together. Simply work a slip stitch into the top of the turning chain at the beginning of the round you have just finished.

Remember that when working in the round, the same side should be facing you throughout.

It's a good idea to use a stitch marker at the beginning of each round as this will help you keep track of where the round stops and starts. Place the stitch marker into the turning chain, and move it up each round as you go.

> *Tip* Each round should end on an increase. If you don't end on an increase, stop and look at your work to find out where the mistake has happened before ripping it out. Finding out where you went wrong will give you a better understanding of how everything fits together.

Front and Back Posts

This technique is used to create a texture by either pushing a stitch forward or backward. It can be used on any stitch but works best on stitches with a visible stem the length of a double crochet and upward. The front and back post technique is used to great effect in the Chunky Chevron Hooded Scarf project (page 32).

Front Post Double Crochet (FPdc)

1 Yarn over, insert your hook (from front to back) around the stitch post one row below, yarn over, and pull up a loop (3 loops on hook).

2 Yarn over and pull through the first 2 loops on your hook (2 loops on hook).

3 Yarn over and pull through the 2 remaining loops on your hook (1 loop on hook).

Front Post Double Crochet Five Together (FPdc5tog)

These stitches are decreased in the same way as a standard double crochet stitch, except for the placement of the hook. The hook is inserted from the back, right to left, in front of the stitch post.

1 Yarn over, insert hook from the back, then around the first stitch post right to left and to the back again. Yarn over and pull back around the stitch (3 loops on hook).

2 Yarn over and pull through first 2 loops on hook (2 loops on hook).

3 Yarn over, insert hook from the back, then around the next stitch post right to left and to the back again. Yarn over and pull back around the stitch (4 loops on hook).

4 Yarn over and pull through first 2 loops on hook (3 loops on hook).

5 Repeat steps 3 and 4 twice more (6 loops on hook).

6 Yarn over and pull through all loops on hook.

Back Post Double Crochet (BPdc)

Yarn over, and insert hook from the front of work, right to left, around the back of the stem (post) of the stitch. Yarn over, and draw the hook back toward yourself. Complete double crochet as normal: yarn over and under two loops, yarn over and under two loops.

You should find that the top of the stitch where you would normally place your hook has been pushed to the back of the work and the stem (post) of the stitch just worked is raised.

Shaping Techniques

Basically, shaping is about adding stitches in and taking them away to create a desired shape. The techniques used are the same for working in rows and for working in the round. A basic beret worked from the top down starts by using the increasing technique until you get to the required width, then moves onto the decreasing techniques to reduce the number of stitches and to bring the shape in to fit the head. When working a flat piece of work in rows, increases and decreases are usually worked at the beginning and end of a row. When working in the round, increasing and decreasing techniques are usually worked in even sections around the outer edge of the work.

Increasing

Internal increases. This is the most straightforward method of adding stitches. Simply work two or more stitches into the same place. This method, when used in rows, is usually worked one or two stitches in from the edge. So, on a row, you would work one stitch, then work your increase, work along the row until you had two or three stitches left, work your increase in the next stitch, and then work one stitch into each until the end.

Adding stitches in this way this gives your work a much neater finish. The increasing marks become a feature of the fabric, and it can also make it easier to sew up.

External increases. This method is used to add several stitches at one time. You do this by adding extra chains at the beginning or end of a row. To add stitches to the beginning of a row using this method, work the required number of chain at the end of the previous row, remembering to add the turning chains. On the next row, work the extra stitches along the chain, and continue working to the end of the row.

To add stitches at the end of a row with this method, work until the last few stitches.

Remove the hook, join a length of yarn to the last stitch on the row, and work the required number of chain. Fasten off the yarn. Place the hook back into the stitch, and continue to work to the end of the row and across the extra chains.

Decreasing

Internal decreases. As with internal increasing, it is best to work this technique at least one stitch in from the edge.

Skip a Stitch

The easiest and most straightforward way to decrease stitches is to simply skip a stitch from the previous row. This is fine when working in single crochet as it is a tight fabric, so skipping one stitch won't show up. But with longer stitches, this method can leave a hole.

Working Stitches Together

With this method, you can work two or more stitches together, and it is used frequently when working more open fabrics.

To work two stitches together, start by working the first stitch of the decrease as you would normally, but do not complete the stitch. Leave the last loop from the stitch on the hook (there should be 2 loops on hook). Work the next stitch from the decrease and, again, do not complete the stitch. Leave the last loop on the hook (3 loops on hook). If you are working more than two together, work every stitch in the decrease as above. Complete the decrease by doing a yarn over and drawing through all the loops on the hook.

External decreases. This method of decreasing is used if you want to decrease a few stitches at the same time. It gives the edges a more angular and stepped effect, so it works better for certain projects.

To work this decrease at the beginning of a row, work a slip stitch into each of the stitches you want to decrease. Then work your turning chain, and continue along the row. To decrease at the end of a row, simply leave the stitches you want to decrease unworked, turn, and continue back along the row.

Crocheting in the Back Loop

A stitch has a front and back loop that meet at one end and look like a horizontal V (looks like this >). To crochet a stitch in the back loop only means you insert the hook under the stitch loop that is away from you and crochet your stitch as usual. This will result in the front loops being left exposed, creating a ridge at the front of your work where you can crochet another row of stitches.

Back Loop Single Crochet

This stitch is worked by inserting the hook under the back loop of the stitch, leaving the front loop showing as a horizontal bar.

1 Chain 1 for turning. Insert hook into the back loop only of the stitch.

2 Yarn over and pull through back loops (2 loops on hook).

3 Yarn over and pull through both loops on hook (1 loop on hook).

Corded Edge

This is a great way of finishing the edges of a project with an attractive border. This is used in the Chunky Chevron Hooded Scarf project (page 32).

1 Start with the hook facing downward, insert the hook from front to back around the post of the first st on the right-hand side.

2 *Yarn over and draw the yarn back through toward yourself, twisting the hook to face upward.

3 Yarn over and draw through both loops on the hook to complete the stitch.

4 Insert the hook into the next space to the right, then repeat from * to end.

Understanding Tension

Tension in both crochet and knitting is the number of stitches and rows it takes to cover a certain area, usually a 4" x 4" (10.2 x 10.2cm) square. However, tension can vary from person to person, even when the same hook and yarn are used, because everybody has their own personal tension. Patterns are written with a specific tension in mind, so if your tension differs from the one given, the finished project will turn out either too big or too small.

Making a Tension Swatch

Always use the recommended hook size and yarn as given in the pattern. Make a piece of crochet fabric between 4" x 4" (10.2 x 10.2cm) and 6" x 6" (15.2 x 15.2cm), making sure you work in the same stitch given in the pattern.

1 Fasten off the yarn. Block and press the piece gently. Lay the sample swatch on a flat surface with the right side facing you. If you are unsure which is the right side, the tail of the chain should be on the left.

2 Place a ruler or tape measure horizontally across the work. Making sure the ruler is straight, use the stitches as a guide. Place pins into the fabric exactly 4" (10.2cm) apart, then count the number of stitches. Include half stitches when counting. Repeat the process vertically to count the rows.

If you are working a stitch pattern, the tension may be given over the pattern repeat rather than the number of stitches and rows. Work the swatch in the pattern, but count the number of pattern repeats between the rows.

Adjusting Your Tension

Often, people don't realize just how important it is getting the tension right. The whole design is based around these numbers, so if you are off even by a little bit, you can end up with a project that is too big or too small. It even affects the number of yarn needed to complete the project, so before you start, it is well worth taking the time to check your tension to avoid any disasters.

> *Tip* If the number of stitches and rows in your swatch matches the pattern, you are ready to start. If you find you have too many stitches or rows, your tension is too tight. Redo the swatch using a larger-sized hook. If you don't have enough stitches, your tension is too loose. Redo the swatch using a smaller-sized hook.

Getting the tension correct for both stitches and rows is equally important, but if you can get the right number of stitches and the rows are slightly off, you can always add rows in or take rows out. The other alternative is to have another look at the size you want to make the finished piece and alter it according to your tension.

Following the Instructions

Finishing Techniques

You can spend all the time in the world getting the stitches and shape correct, but if the finish doesn't look good, it can really spoil the look of the finished product. It's exciting when you get to this stage, but try not to rush it.

Fastening Off

Once you have completed your last stitch, you need to secure the yarn to stop it all from unravelling. This is called fastening off or binding off. Cut the yarn, leaving approx. 4"–6" (10.2–15.2cm) yarn. Draw the loose end through the last loop on the hook and pull tightly to secure.

Sewing in Loose Ends

Before blocking and pressing a project, it's best to sew in all the loose ends. You will need to use a tapestry needle, which has a large eye and a rounded end. Thread the needle and weave the ends in by running it through the stitches nearest to the loose ends. It's easiest to do this with the work inside out, otherwise the outer seams can look bulky.

Blocking and Pressing

Before sewing up, you need to make sure all the pieces are the correct size and shape. To block a piece of crochet, pin the pieces onto a padded surface. An ironing board will do for smaller pieces, but you may need to improvise for larger pieces—a wooden board with a few layers of quilter's batting covered with a checkered fabric tea towel is ideal. The check pattern helps you to keep the edges straight, and the fabric itself will protect the surface from the iron.

Always check the yarn ball band for care instructions. If it has a high synthetic-fiber content, do not go near it with the iron as it will stretch out of shape or, at worst, will melt with the heat. Pin the pieces right side down on the padded surface using glass-headed pins. Ease the crochet into shape, then check its measurements against the pattern. For natural fibers, place a damp towel over the work and gently hover the iron over at a steam setting. For synthetic fibers or yarns with a high synthetic content, spray the fabric lightly with water. Do not go near it with a dry or a steam iron as the heat will make the fabric lose its shape. Allow to dry before removing the pins.

Understanding Patterns

When you first look at a crochet pattern, it can look a bit like a foreign language, so it's best to start off with a simple one and build up to something more complicated. It's also good to get into the habit of checking you have the correct number of stitches at the end of each row or round, and it's best to work through the instructions exactly as they are given.

Following the Pattern

Most patterns are written as repeats, which are indicated in parentheses and with asterisks. It is very important to pay attention to these, along with the commas and periods. You will also find that the correct number of stitches, if there have been any increases or decreases in the row, are shown in closed parentheses at the end of each row or round.

> **Tip** All patterns give you information about the project at the beginning. It will tell you what materials you will need, as well as the finished size and any pattern abbreviations. It's important to read through these carefully before you start because they may include a variation of a technique that is important to that specific design.

Seams

There are a few methods of sewing your crochet together, depending on the type of seam you want and the type of project you are making. Pieces can be joined together either by sewing with a large-eyed blunt needle or by using a crochet hook. Generally, it is a matter of personal preference, whereby you use the method that you are most comfortable with and gives you the best finish, but sometimes a pattern will ask for a specific type of seam.

Joining Stitches at the Sides

When joining the front and back of a project together, you can join them almost invisibly together.

- Lay the two crochet pieces side by side, and pin together with safety pins. Match up the top and bottom first, then the center points. You'll find that even though you have worked the same number of rows for each piece, there is still a slight difference in the length; however, by pinning the pieces together in this way, you can easily absorb any slight differences.
- Thread the sewing needle with a length of yarn. Try to use the same yarn that the project has been worked in, or if it's not suitable, go for a yarn that tones into the fabric well. Bring the needle up from back to front, starting from the bottom-right stitch on the left-hand piece, and pull the needle through, leaving a 4"–6" (10.2–15.2cm) tail.
- Place the needle from back to front, starting from the bottom-left stitch on the right-hand piece, pulling the yarn through, and drawing the two pieces of fabric together. Repeat the process once more. Work into the bottom stitches, creating a figure eight, and pulling the yarn tight as you go. The yarn will now be secure, and you should have an even, straight edge.

The process for working up the side seam differs slightly according to the stitch used for the fabric. For single crochet (sc), you should zigzag between the tops of the stitches. For double crochet (dc), zigzag between the top, middle, and bottom of the stitches.

- Bring the needle up through the post of the first stitch on the left-hand side, and then do the same for the opposite side. Zigzagging back and forth, insert the needle into the same place you came out of, but move directly up one stitch each time. You will sometimes be joining stitches to turning chains, but don't worry too much about where your needle is coming out of—just try to keep everything even.
- After you have worked three or four rows, gently pull on the yarn to draw the two seams together. They should link up evenly and be more or less flat. When you reach the top, secure the yarn by working a few times through the top stitches and weave in the loose end before trimming.

Joining Tops Together

The way you join the tops of two crochet pieces together is similar to the method for joining the sides. Lay the pieces next to one another and pin together. This time, however, instead of working into the stitches or turning chains, you will be joining the tops of the stitches together.

- With the right sides of the fabric facing you, secure the yarn at the beginning of the seam using the figure eight method as described before. Start by inserting your needle into the bottommost outer loop on the left-hand side, then cross over to the bottommost loop on the right-hand side. Pull firmly and repeat.
- Work along the rest of the seam. Insert your needle from back to front, coming up through the center of the first V on the left-hand side. Move the needle across to the right-hand side, and insert the needle

into the place that the yarn came out from the last figure eight loop. Pull the needle out through the center of the next V on the same side, and zigzag back and forth like this until you reach the end of the seam. Secure the yarn by working a final figure eight loop.

Joining Tops to Sides

Joining the top of one piece to the side of another piece uses a combination of the two methods. Stitches are often longer than they are wide, so they don't always match up with each other exactly. As you will be working through either the stem of a stitch or the center of a turning chain, it is especially important to pin pieces together when joining tops to sides.

Backstitch

Certain projects need a sturdy nonstretch seam, which is more about functionality than beauty. For projects like Outdoor Cushion (page 36), backstitch is perfect. To join two pieces together using backstitch, have the right sides facing to the inside and pin together, making sure the rows and stitches match up evenly.

- Secure the yarn to the right-hand side of the seam by working a few small stitches on top of one another through both layers of the fabric. Insert the needle back into the fabric at the beginning of the seam, and draw through to the wrong side. Move the needle up a centimeter or so along the back of the work, and bring the needle back through to the right side, pulling the yarn tight.
- *Insert the needle back into the end of the last stitch worked. Move up the seam a centimeter or so, and bring the needle

through to the right side, pulling tight. Keep repeating from the * to the end of the seam. Secure the end by working a few stitches on top of one another.

Crocheting Seams Together

Seams can also be crocheted together. It is very straightforward and easy to do but does leave a visible seam, and the seam is rather bulky, so do take this into consideration.

- Place your pieces together either with right sides or wrong sides facing, depending on if you want the seam to be on the inside or outside of your work. Pin together, making sure that the stitches and rows match up and the ends meet. Insert your hook through both pieces of fabric on the right-hand side at the very outer edge. Make a slip knot, pop it on your hook, and draw the hook back through toward yourself.
- If you are working a slip stitch seam, *insert your hook into the next stitch through both pieces of fabric, yarn over, and draw back through (2 loops on hook). Draw the first loop under the second loop, and repeat from * until seam is complete. Cut yarn, leaving approx. 4"–6" (10.2–15.2cm) length, yarn over the loose end, and pull through to secure.
- If you are working a single crochet seam, yarn over and draw through. *Insert your hook into the next stitch through both pieces of fabric, yarn over, draw back through (2 loops on hook), yarn over again, and draw through both loops. Repeat from * until seam is complete. Cut yarn, leaving approx. 4"–6" (10.2–15.2cm) length, yarn over the loose end, and pull through to secure.

A similar effect to backstitch can be made using a crochet hook.

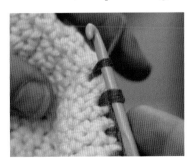

Crocheted seams can be made on the inside or outside of the project.

The Projects

Narrow Stripe Beret

This beautifully soft beret is a good project to tackle once you are confident with the basic stitches. It is worked in the round throughout, so there are no seams to sew up. This hat can also be worked in a single color to avoid those fiddly color changes. Make this hat and think of trips to the seaside, lots of fresh air, and sand between your toes!

Finished Size
22" (56cm) circumference around band

Materials
Yarn: Blue Sky Fibers Baby Alpaca, fine weight, 100% alpaca, 109 yards (100m) per 1.8oz (50g) ball
   A—Natural White x 2
   B—Bleu Cheese x 1
   C—Cornflower x 1
Hook: US G/6 (4mm)

Tension
Using size G/6 (4mm) hook, approx. 20 sts and 19 rows over 4" x 4" (10.2 x 10.2cm) square of single crochet

Abbreviations
Sc2tog—single crochet 2 together
See also page 40

Using size G/6 (4mm) hook and yarn A, work 5ch, sl st into first ch to make a ring.

Round 1: 1ch, PM (place marker), work 10sc into ring, sl st into 1ch at beg of round. (10 sts)

Move place marker, and put it after 1ch worked at the beginning of each round.

Round 2: 1ch, work 2sc into the back loop of first sc, *2sc into back loop of next sc, rep from * to end, sl st into 1ch at beg of round. (20 sts)

Change to yarn B—place yarn B over hook and pull through loop already on hook. Pull yarn A tight so loop disappears into work.

Work into back loop of every sc throughout.

Round 3: 1ch, work 1sc into first sc, 2sc into next sc, *1sc into next sc, 2sc into next sc, rep from * to end, sl st into 1ch at beg of round. (30 sts)

Change to yarn A—as described above.

Round 4: 1ch, work 1sc into first and every following st to end, sl st into 1ch at beg of round. (30 sts)

Change to yarn C.

Round 5: 1ch, work 1sc into first 2sc, 2sc into next sc, *1sc into next 2sc, 2sc into next sc, rep from * to end, sl st into 1ch at beg of round. (40 sts)

Change to yarn A.

Round 6: 1ch, work 1sc into first and every following st to end, sl st into 1ch at beg of round. (40 sts)

Change to yarn B.

Round 7: 1ch, work 1sc into first 3sc, 2sc into next sc, *1sc into next 3sc, 2sc into next sc, rep from * to end, sl st into 1ch at beg of round. (50 sts)

Change to yarn A.

Round 8: 1ch, work 1sc into first and every following st to end, sl st into 1ch at beg of round. (50 sts)

Change to yarn C.

Round 9: 1ch, work 1sc into first 4sc, 2sc into next sc, *1sc into next 4sc, 2sc into next sc, rep from * to end, sl st into 1ch at beg of round. (60 sts)

Keep the stripe sequence throughout as established in rounds 6–9.

Keep the shaping sequence correct by adding 1 onto the number of sc worked before increasing (working 2sts into same stitch) on next and every second row until there are 140 sts (12 sts between increasing).

Before starting decrease, gently block and press top of beret.

Rounds 26–28: 1ch, work 1sc into first and every following st to end, sl st into 1ch at beg of round. (140 sts)

Round 29: 1ch, *1sc into next 12sc, sc2tog, rep from * to end. (130 sts)

Round 30: 1ch, work 1sc into first and every following st to end, sl st into 1ch at beg of round. (130 sts)

Round 31: 1ch, *1sc into next 11sc, sc2tog, rep from * to end. (120 sts)

Round 32: 1ch, work 1sc into first and every following st to end, sl st into 1ch at beg of round. (120 sts)

Round 33: 1ch, *1sc into next 10sts, sc2tog, rep from * to end. (110 sts)

Round 34: 1ch, work 1sc into first and every following st to end, sl st into 1ch at beg of round. (110 sts)

Round 35: 1ch, *1sc into next 9sc, sc2tog, rep from * to end. (100 sts)

Round 36: 1ch, work 1sc into first and every following st to end, sl st into 1ch at beg of round. (100 sts)

Round 37: 1ch, *1sc into next 8sc, sc2tog, rep from * to end. (90 sts)

Round 38: 1ch, work 1sc into first and every following st to end, sl st into 1ch at beg of round. (90 sts)

Round 39: 1ch, *1sc into next 7sc, sc2tog, rep from * to end. (80 sts)

Round 40: 1ch, work 1sc into first and every following st to end, sl st into 1ch at beg of round. (80 sts)

Round 41: 1ch, *1sc into next 6sc, sc2tog, rep from * to end. (70 sts)

Work 7 rounds in yarn A and 1 round in yarn C, as done in Row 40.

Cut yarn and fasten off.

Finishing

Sew in loose ends to inside of hat.

Chunky Chevron Hooded Scarf

Is it a scarf? Is it a hood? No, it's both! This two-in-one design will keep your head and neck snugly wrapped up from the winter chill. Worked in a wool and bulky-weight yarn, it's super soft next to the skin. The chevron stitch will keep your interest as you work through the panels, and the corded trim adds the perfect finishing touch.

Finished Size
Width: 10½" (26.7cm); Length: 52½" (133.4cm) at hood

Materials
Yarn: Patons Classic Wool Roving, bulky weight, 100% wool, 120 yards (109m) per 3.5oz (100g) ball

    Aran x 6

Hooks: US G/6 (4mm) and US J/10 (6mm)

Tension
Using size J/10 (6mm) hook, approx. 12 sts and 6 rows over 4" x 4" (10.2 x 10.2cm) square of double crochets

Abbreviations
FPdc—double crochet around front post

FPdc5tog—double crochet 5 together around front post

See also page 40

Left Scarf Panel

Using size J/10 (6mm) hook, make 37ch.

Row 1: 1ch, 1sc into second ch from hook, 1sc into each ch to end. (37 sts)

Row 2: 2ch, 1dc into first st, 3dc into next st, 1dc into next 14 sts, dc5tog over next 5 sts, 1dc into next 14 sts, 3dc into next st, 1dc into last st, turn.

Rows 3–6: Repeat Row 2.

Row 7: 2ch, 1dc into first st, 2FPdc into next st, 1FPdc into next 14 sts, FPdc5tog over next 5 sts, 1FPdc into next 14 sts, 2FPdc into next st, 1dc into last st, turn. (35 sts)

Row 8: 2ch, 1dc into first st, 3dc into next st,1dc into next 13 sts, dc5tog over next 5 sts, 1dc into next 13 sts, 3dc into next st, 1dc into last st, turn.

Rows 9–10: Repeat Row 8.

Row 11: 2ch, 1dc into first st, 1FPdc into next 14 sts, FPdc5tog over next 5 sts, 1FPdc into next 14 sts, 1dc into last st, turn. (31 sts)

Row 12: 2ch, 1dc into first st, 3dc into next st, 1dc into next 11 sts, dc5tog over next 5 sts, 1dc into next 11 sts, 3dc into next st, 1dc into last st, turn.

Rows 13–14: Repeat Row 12.

Row 15: 2ch, 1dc into first st, 3FPdc into next st, 1FPdc into next 11 sts, FPdc5tog over next 5 sts, 1FPdc into next 11 sts, 3FPdc into next st, 1dc into last st, turn.

Row 16: 2ch, 1dc into first st, 3dc into next st, 1dc into next 11 sts, dc5tog over next 5 sts, 1dc into next 11 sts, 3dc into next st, 1dc into last st, turn.

Rows 17–18: Repeat Row 16.

Row 19: 2ch, 1dc into first st, 1FPdc into next 12 sts, FPdc5tog over next 5 sts, 1FPdc into next 12 sts, 1dc into last st, turn. (27 sts)

Row 20: 2ch, 1dc into first st, 3dc into next st, 1dc into next 9 sts, dc5tog over next 5 sts, 1dc into next 9 sts, 3dc into next st, 1dc into last st, turn.

Rows 21–22: Repeat Row 20.

Row 23: 2ch, 1dc into first st, 3FPdc into next st, 1FPdc into next 9 sts, FPdc5tog over next 5 sts, 1FPdc into next 9 sts, 3FPdc into next st, 1dc into last st, turn.

Rows 24–26: Repeat Row 20.

Row 27: Repeat Row 23.

Repeat Rows 24–27, five more times.

Row 48: Repeat Row 23.

**Shape for hood by increasing on first half of chevron and keeping pattern correct on second half, as follows:

Row 49 (inc): 2ch, 1dc into first st, 3dc into next st, 1dc into next 11 sts, dc3tog over next 3 sts, 1dc into next 9 sts, 3dc into next st, 1dc into last st. (29 sts)

Row 50: 2ch, 1dc into first st, 3dc into next st, 1dc into next 9 sts, dc3tog over next 3 sts, 1dc into each st to end, turn.

Row 51 (inc): 2ch, 1dc into first st, 3FPdc into next st, 1FPdc into next 13 sts, dc3tog over next 3 sts, 1FPdc into next 9 sts, 1 FPdc into next st, 1dc into last st, turn. (31 sts)

Row 52: 2ch, 1dc into first st, 3dc into next st, 1dc into next 9 sts, dc3tog over next 3 sts, 1dc into each st to end, turn.

Row 53: 2ch, 1dc into each st to end, turn.

Row 54: Repeat Row 53.

Row 55: 2ch, 1dc into first st, 1FPdc into each st to end, turn.

Row 56: Repeat Row 53.

Repeat last 4 rows 3 more times, then Rows 53–54 once more.

Cut yarn and fasten off.

Right Scarf Panel

Work as directed in Left Scarf Panel until **

Shape the hood by keeping pattern correct on the first half and increasing on second half of chevron as follows:

Row 49 (inc): 2ch, 1dc into first st, 3dc into next st, 1dc into next 9 sts, dc3tog over next 3 sts, 1dc into next 11 sts, 3dc into next st, 1dc into last st. (29 sts)

Row 50: 2ch, 1dc into first st, 3dc into next st, 1dc into next 11 sts, dc3tog over next 3 sts, 1dc into each st to end, turn.

Row 51 (inc): 2ch, 1dc into first st, 3FPdc into next st, 1FPdc into next 9 sts, dc3tog over next 3 sts, 1FPdc into next 13 sts, 1 FPdc into next st, 1dc into last st, turn. (31 sts)

Row 52: 2ch, 1dc into first st, 3dc into next st, 1dc into next 15 sts, dc3tog over next 3 sts, 1dc into each st to end, turn.

Row 53: 2ch, 1dc into each st to end, turn.

Row 54: Repeat Row 53.

Row 55: 2ch, 1dc into first st, 1FPdc into each st to end, turn.

Row 56: Repeat Row 53.

Repeat last 4 rows 3 more times, then Rows 53–54 once more.

Cut yarn and fasten off.

Finishing

Sew in all loose ends, block, and press scarf panels.

Using a backstitch, sew the top of the hood panels together, then sew the back seam of the hood from the start of head shaping. **Work corded reverse sc trim around outer edge of scarf:**

With right side facing and using US G/6 (4mm) hook, rejoin yarn to center seam at the back of the hood. Start with the hook facing downward, insert the hook from front to back around the post of the first st on the right-hand side. *Yarn over, and draw the yarn back through toward yourself, twisting the hook to face upward. Yarn over, and draw through both loops on the hook to complete the stitch. Insert the hook into the next space to the right, rep from * to end around the outer edge of scarf and hood, sl st into first st.

Cut yarn and fasten off. Sew in loose ends.

Outdoor Cushion

This cushion is perfect for lazy summer afternoons in your backyard or even to take on a picnic. Tweed is ideal for outdoor use.

Finished Size
18" x 18" (45.7 x 45.7cm)

Materials
Yarn: Lion Brand Re-Tweed, medium weight, 40% wool/40% polyester/20% acrylic, 202 yards (185m) per 3.5oz (100g) ball

    A—Everglade x 1
    B—Peanut Butter x 1

Buttons x 4
Hook: US G/6 (4mm)

Tension
Using size G/6 (4mm) hook, approx. 19 sts and 16 rows over 4" x 4" (10.2 x 10.2cm) square of pattern

Abbreviations
See page 40

Textured Squares

Make 4 in yarn A and 4 in yarn B.

Using size G/6 (4mm) hook, make 39ch.

Row 1: 1ch, 1sc into second ch from hook, 1sc into each ch to end, turn. (39sts)

Row 2: 1ch, 1sc into first sc, *1ch, skip 1sc, 1sc into next sc, rep from * to end, turn.

Row 3: 2 ch, skip first sc, 1sc into first ch sp, *1ch, skip next sc, 1sc into next ch sp, rep from * to first, 1sc into last sc, turn.

Row 4: 1ch, 1sc into first sc, *1ch, skip 1sc, 1sc into next sc, rep from * to end.

Repeat last 2 rows 13 times, then Row 3 once more.

Next row: 1ch, 1sc into first sc, *1sc into ch sp, 1sc into next sc, rep from * to end.

Cut yarn and fasten off.

Cushion Flap

Make 1 in yarn A and 1 in yarn B.

Work as directed in Textured Squares for Rows 1–3.

Place buttonholes.

Row 4: 1ch, skip first sc, 1sc into ch sp, (1ch, skip 1sc, 1sc into next ch sp) 3 times, 3ch, skip (1sc, 1ch sp and 1sc) (1sc into next ch sp, 1ch, skip 1sc) 9 times, 2ch, skip (1ch sp and 1sc) *1sc into next ch sp, 1ch, skip 1sc, rep from * to end, working last sc into tch at end of row, turn.

Repeat Row 3 from Textured Squares 10 more times.

Next row: 1ch, 1sc into first sc, *1sc into ch sp, 1sc into next sc, rep from * to end.

Cut yarn and fasten off.

Finishing

Sew in all loose ends.

Block and press squares.

Make up front and back cushion panels as follows:

Using the photo as a guide, make check pattern with four squares, and stitch together using back stitch; the seams are to the right side for a decorative finish.

Sew base and side seams together, leaving top open. Sew two flap rectangles together, then stitch to front panel. Sew buttons onto back panel to match up with buttonholes.

Index

adjusting your tension, 22
animal fibers, 10

back loop single crochet, 20–21
back post double crochet, 18
backstitch, 25
Basic stitch techniques, 12–15
  counting chains, 13
  double crochet, 15
  making a foundation chain,
    12–13
  making the first loop, 12
  single crochet, 14
  slip stitch, 13
  turning chains, 13
blocking and pressing, 23

chains, 13
  counting
  turning
"Chunky Chevron Hooded
  Scarf," 32–35
corded edge, 21
Crochet Hook Conversion
  Chart, 40
crocheting in the back loop,
  20–21
  back loop single crochet
crocheting seams together, 25
counting chains, 13

decreasing, 19–20
double crochet, 15

fastening off, 23
finishing techniques, 23
Following the instructions, 23
  blocking and pressing
  fastening off
  finishing techniques
  sewing in loose ends
following the pattern, 23
front and back posts, 17–18
  back post double crochet, 18
  front post double crochet, 17
  front post double crochet five
    together, 17–18
front post double crochet, 17

front post double crochet five
  together, 17–18

Getting started, 11
  holding the hook
  holding the yarn

holding the hook, 11
holding the yarn, 11
hooks, 8

increasing, 19
increasing in the round, 16

joining stitches at the sides, 24
joining tops to sides, 25
joining tops together, 24

making a foundation chain,
  12–13
making a tension swatch, 22
making a ring, 16
making the first loop, 12

"Narrow Stripe Beret," 28–31

"Outdoor Cushion," 36–38

pins, 8–9
plant fibers, 10
Projects, 26–38
  "Chunky Chevron Hooded
    Scarf," 32–35
  "Narrow Stripe Beret," 28–31
  "Outdoor Cushion," 36–38

scissors, 9
Seams, 24–25
  backstitch, 25
  crocheting seams together, 25
  joining stitches at the sides, 24
  joining tops to sides, 25
  joining tops together, 24
sewing in loose ends, 23
sewing needles, 9
Shaping techniques, 19–20
  decreasing, 19–20
  increasing, 19

single crochet, 14
slip stitch, 13
stitch markers, 9
synthetic fibers, 10

Table of Abbreviations, 40
tape measure, 9
The Basics, 6–25
  Basic stitch techniques, 12–15
  corded edge, 21
  Crocheting in the back loop,
    20–21
  Following the instructions, 23
  Front and back posts, 17–18
  Getting started, 11
  Seams, 24–25
  Shaping techniques, 19–20
  Tools, 8–9
  Understanding patterns, 23
  Understanding tension, 22
  Working in the round, 16
  Yarns, 10
Tools, 8–9
  hooks, 8
  pins, 8–9
  scissors, 9
  sewing needles, 9
  stitch markers, 9
  tape measure, 9
turning chains, 13

Understanding patterns, 23
  following the pattern
Understanding tension, 22
  adjusting your tension
  making a tension swatch

Working in the round, 16
  increasing in the round
  making a ring
  working into the ring
working into the ring, 16

Yarns, 10
  animal fibers
  plant fibers
  synthetic fibers

Crochet Hook Conversion Chart		
Metric	**US**	**Old UK**
1.75mm	5 or 6	15 or 2½ or 3
2mm	1 or B	14 or 1½ or 1
2.5mm	2 or C	12 or 0 or 2/0
3mm	3 or D	10 or 11 or 3/0
3.5mm	4 or E	9
4mm	5 or F	8
4.5mm	6 or G	7
5mm	8 or H	6
5.5mm	9 or I	5
6mm	10 or J	4
6.5mm	10½ or K	3
7mm	No equivalent	2
7.5mm	No equivalent	1
8mm	11 or L	0
9mm	13 or M	00
10mm	15 or N	000
12mm	16 or O	No equivalent

Table of Abbreviations	
Beg	beginning
BPdc	back post double crochet
Ch	chain
Ch sp	chain space
Dc	double crochet
Dc2tog	double crochet 2 together
Dc3tog	double crochet 3 together
Dc4tog	double crochet 4 together
Dc5tog	double crochet 5 together
FPdc	front post double crochet
FPdc3tog	double crochet 3 together around front of stem (post)
FPdc5tog	double crochet 5 together around front of stem (post)
PM	place marker
Rep	repeat
Sc	single crochet
Sc2tog	single crochet 2 together
Sl st	slip stitch
Tch	turning chain
Tog	together
Yo	yarn over